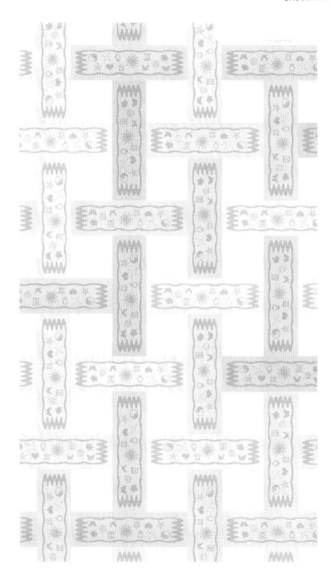

Elemental Poems

Of Being. Of the Mind. Of the Heart.

John Deed

Published by John Deed, Thriplow, England

www.flyingpigments.co.uk

ISBN 978-1-8382787-2-4
Text and image copyright © John Deed, 2021

To Carol

For love and guidance.

Maps and compass in hand all the way!

&

My family

For always giving me hope

of what might be at the next port.

&

All those who have come on board

from time to time to help me sail this ship.

In memory of Cal

Index

Part 1. Elements of Being

Part 2. Elements of the Mind (Journey to a Void)

Part 3. Elements of the Heart

Introduction

I grew up in relatively fortunate surroundings in rural England. For most of my adult life I have had a regular job and, with a loving family, I count my blessings in this respect.

This is a book of poems, but I wouldn't consider myself either a poet or a literary scholar. However, I enjoy words and the possibilities that words possess - to paint a picture, to summarise a situation or to convey a hidden feeling. Rhyme, rhythm, flow. Irony, juxtaposition, antilogy. Contrast, boundary, tension.

Stations names of inspiration on my journey over the years have been many and varied; from Shakespeare to Hardy and from Dylan to Costello, with plenty more minor stops of everyday life in-between.

When writing, I tend to make a note of thoughts or snippets or daydreams as they occur, which may then lay dormant for some while before erupting into something more structured. Anyhow, the result is this collection, formed from personal experience or observation (is there a difference?) which I would like to share with you.

Why? Putting to one side any hubris of "because I can" or the vanity of wanting someone to like them, if I can spark a thought, an idea, a conversation or create some resonance that will be sufficient.

Part 1.

Elements of Being

Most of my more grounded moments are when interacting with the natural world, unique moments in space and time. This might be a physical observation of some majestic vista or the impossible intricacy of the simplest flower.

Or a memory of how the great machinery that drives these magical marvels keeps grinding on regardless, whilst we go about our busy lives.

Or wondering what will become of the natural order in the course of time, our ephemeral place in this scheme and our influence, good or bad, upon it.

Or the imponderable which is whether fate or some greater force makes things so.

Awakening

The sky's lid slowly opened
And revealed a watery blue eye
With thin crimson veins
It looked pale and tired
Against the lark that rose up to fly.

5 a.m.

I wake up early
To hear the sunrise
To see the dawn chorus
To touch transient skies
To smell the plump berries
To taste the heady air of corn
I wake up early
To come alive.

The Little Things

From outer space we are another world
Utopian sphere-swirling whirligig
A hurdy-gurdy journey through space and time
Clouds, oceans, ice caps, deserts and pastures green
A globe, a play, the sum of all its parts
Made much greater from myriad acts unseen

Looking closer, this place just titled "Earth"
Reveals an unimaginable tale
Conceived with an infinite inspiration
A trillion chapters written every second
Each chapter crafted with a million words
War and peace, an epic story reckoned

But it's a fragile orb that needs much care
To be a place wonderous to discover
Not to be a tome that's only a cover
A perfect planet with beating heart and soul
Remember that it's all the little things
That meld and fuse to form this wondrous whole

It's in our hands the way which we direct
Each a trusted steward of the script
Subtext tapestry of things we do or say
To that extent we all have equal voices
To make acts of kindness and acts of love
Final fabric woven from our choices.

Ponder

May your mind always wander and wonder
Let it enquire within and without
Though certainty needs no courage
I have found at some length
The fuel of existence is doubt

Mighty mountains are made at the boundaries
Volcanoes explode through thin crust
Angels are seen after dark
Fires ignite from a spark
Stars form from a ferment of dust

Take time to stare into infinity
Ponder the order of all far and wide
And if your questions should cease
After a moment's brief peace
Your ephemeral soul will have died.

All in Good Time

The acorn gives rise to
Boughs mighty and tall
So, all creatures great
Begin beautifully small

After much tender care
Full grapes fill the vine
Picked plump and matured
For a velvety wine

Like the new born kitten
That longs for first sight
Owl in its wisdom
Sits tight for the night

Fruit forms the flower
On the apple tree
Ice melts on the hill
Before reaching the sea

Just as the sun rises
Summer follows spring
Chrysalis conceals
Splendid swallowtail wings

The ewe expects to love
Her new lamb within
Enjoy the freedom
Of the moments you're in

Cherish shiny mornings
Make the present last
One day you'll call time
When change happens too fast

Keep on with your journey
Keep up your sweet smile
One inch at a time
As you walk the long mile.

Tuscan Senses

The clatter of the tractor
On the sun-baked Tuscan hills
A golden blanket folded
Round the earth the farmer tills

Overhead an eagle slides
Majestic, silent drama
Ruthless purpose as she views
A perfect panorama

Bells ring out upon the air
From the distant, creamy fleece
Doves coo on the pantiled roof
High above the hissing geese

The grapes grow in the vineyard
Inky, plump and gorged with juice
Freed then corked then free again
Rich, deep flavours bursting loose

I walk on through the pastures
With the dirt beneath my feet
So soft and warm and sensual
Bedding to the aurous wheat

And the dusty track is lined
By saluting cypress trees
Which at dusk give up their scent
To the gentle evening breeze.

———————————————————

Normandy Woods

As I walk through the ancient fern
With a racing future mind
Hoping to slow up just enough
Osiris secrets to find

Where I can see the dragonfly dart
Across the leafy forest floor
Just as over yonder clearing
Two falcons stretch and soar

I look forward from my memory
To a place in space and time
Where nature's numbers all add up
And all her words will rhyme

The season's beat in the farmer's vein
Flows in rhythmic harmony
And from the chaos of the winds
Comes steadfast certainty.

- - - - - - - - - - - - - - - - - - -

Two Drops

A perfect drop
That fell from Heaven
Made the moisture
In the viper's venom
The next it fell upon the bough
That grew the leaf
That fed the cow
That made the milk for my morning drink
And as I sipped
It made me think
About the infinite plan of the Maker
Life giver and life taker.

Titanic

Innocent with milky muzzle
Mother's offspring ends its nuzzle
Sweet warm breath of the new born fawn
Warmed the air of the frosty morn
Some condensed on its mother's nose
The rest dispersed and lightly rose
Drawn by the sun to the sky beyond
Vapour found vapour and formed a bond
Blown by the wind as gossamer shroud
Miles away into darker clouds
Then northward bound for days on end
Like silent ships their way did wend
Ever onwards the fleet drove harder
All-advancing airborne armada
Soon from the west and joining forces
A thousand black sky-riding horses
Every last drop conscripted there
Had left its donor unaware
Some cast aside when it lightly rained
The rest locked in their fate pre-ordained.
Over stormy seas and hostile land
Each cloud's cloak concealed a sleight of hand
For many days it took to make
The perfect form of each snowflake
Each drop transformed, not one with flaws
All obeying universal laws

Facets and fronds exquisitely formed
(And yes, the drops the fawn had warmed)
Pregnant nimbus now fit to burst
Crack of lightning, the wizard cursed
Without warning in the dead of night
Millions were born dressed in virgin white
Slowly swirling towards the ground
Settling softly without a sound
And in a moment, no-one to wonder
Were covered up and laid asunder
Layer on layer, no favour no fault
Fates sealed in an Arctic vault
Hardening by millennia once, twice, thrice
Transformed into a sea of ice
That creaked and groaned so plaintively
Hour by long hour to destiny
And finally, ice met the ocean
An unknown hour, untold commotion
Only timed by nature's clock
There calved a vast unwieldy block
Cast adrift like a rudderless boat
Chilling the seas, barely able to float
But move it did, leaving no clues
Of a destiny it did not choose.
Meanwhile, into warmer waters slipped
A black behemoth, mother of ships

Epitome of man's endeavour
Mix of muscle and brains so clever
Every last rivet so perfectly planned
She sailed with cheers for a far-off land
Now, there were two hulks sailing in rhyme
Destined to share the same space and time
One sent with engines, charts and compass
One chillingly slid to the impasse
One alive with orchestra playing
One lifeless, ready for the slaying
Both though part of an elaborate plan
Nature collides with the wit of man
And in the relative blink of an eye
One would live and one would die
But for all man's earthly command
He cannot beat fate's winning hand
Fifteen hundred sent to their death
By nothing more than a newborn's breath.

Hour Glass

Everyone's got their own hour glass
Quietly emptying in a darkened room
No-one knows how much time it contains
Until lit by a soft and silvery moon.

Then at this moment of enlightenment
Whether a second a month or a year
Each grain now precious as a diamond
Every moment immeasurably dear.
Do we need to see it to believe it?
Always knowing it will empty some day
Why can't we love each breath as if finite?
Live like the silence of the void was near
Do we worry that we'd make constant merry?
Become shallow and forget who we are?
Fear not!
You'll shine with kindness and wisdom
Finding inner peace, not inner war.

15

Brothers in Arms

A dusty yard, a summer breeze
A soothing rustle from the trees
Two brothers play with wooden hoops
Delighted yelps and joyous whoops
There are no finer days than these

And then the sound that both boys dread
Mother scolding, "You'll wake the dead!"
Heavy hearts they know their duty
She takes in this scene of beauty
Cold wash, warm hugs, it's time for bed

Dad calls out as they climb the stairs:
"And don't forget to say your prayers!".
"What'll you be when you're older?"
"I want to be a brave soldier"
"Me too", then night dissolves their cares

Years roll by and brotherhood binds
Limbs lengthened, strengthened, paths entwined
Boyhood, manhood, graduation
The peak of life's expectation
A world awaits, its wonders to find

Then one day they awake once more
Rat-a-tat-tat a knock at the door

Mother, father rush to see
Three tall men from the military
"We've come to take your sons to war"

Archibald and Bernard get dressed
Their shirts are ironed, their trousers pressed
"Don't fret" they say "We need to sign"
Ink like blood on a dotted line
Brave faced parents: "May you be blessed"

For King and Country, they've now signed
Unwritten chapters left behind
In unison they cry out loud
"Mother, father we'll make you proud!"
Cheery smiles conceal worried minds

One joins the Rifles for the war
The other's in the Machine Gun Corps
Shipped away on a packet boat
Shiny boots and a khaki coat
To live or die on foreign shores

Brothers now are Belgian and French
Home a funk-hole, bivvy, trench
Shared experience but miles apart
No end, no middle and no start
Incessant roar and rotten stench

Under a blue, benevolent sky
Coal boxes, crumps and stick bombs fly
Comrades rise and sink like the sun
Both bricks and mortars fall as one
Ypres, Thiepval, Arras, Cambrai

Father paces while mother sews
"Home sweet home" as the saying goes
Carelessly she pricks her thumb
A drop of blood, her mind goes numb
Just as two shots are fired by foes

From hot dark confines of the gun
For fractions fizzing in the sun
Just as the maker had designed
Soft fleshy targets both do find
Brothers in arms now brothers one

Bernard thwarts his enemy ace
Thanks be for his spectacles case
Archibald though has no such luck
Host to death's wish the bullet struck
Fate's crossroad of wrong time wrong place

Bereft, Bernard drifts home alone
Archibald "Whereabouts unknown"

Peace returns served with joy with grief
Life's line cut by a faceless thief
Brother, son in some muddy tomb

For all it's been a long hard road
For Bernard the shells still explode
For mum the baking tray's too wide
For dad he slides one glass aside
For one life's hopes like blood have flowed:

Like taking rest after travail
To strive for dreams, succeed or fail
Sharing laughter round the table
Fact or farce or family fable
Life's daily detail to regale

Soft summer cotton drenched in rain
The deepest cuts of love and pain
Keep a secret nobody knows
Cool sea and sand between the toes
Harvest aroma, ripened grain

Lie heavenwards, watch clouds float by
Springtime blossoming, lover's sigh
Swelling fruits from the orchard's trees
Taste sweet honey from busy bees
Hear a baby's primal cry

Sadly, I knew just one brother
Fate chose one and not the other
But for deadly hands dealt by chance
His line, too, could have stopped in France
Great War soldier, not great grandfather

And who should I thank for it all?
The one that lived? The one to fall?
The maker of the glasses case?
The enemy's forgotten face?
Just thank God I can thank at all.

Concrete Planet

Earth, earth, Mother Earth
Formed countless aeons ago
Laws of physics, laws of God
There's nothing you don't know

Air, water, verdant life
Intertwined for a greater whole
Constantly evolving
Checked and balanced to that goal

Ant, auk, great white shark
Unique but dependent so
The gyroscope of nature
Tilts if one should shrink or grow

Dynamic equilibrium
Constant change 'gainst constant force
All form held to account
Weeping willow or wild white horse

Then came man with grand ideas
With brains to beat the brawn
Slash the trees and spray the bees
Apparent king to nature's pawn

But the brains were still connected
To selfish survival genes
I want, I can, I will
Concrete jungle buries green

Time will tell how smart we are
And what our being will bring
As each small step ratchets up
The eternal reckoning spring

Great walls and shiny towers
Follies of independence
We are all irrevocably bound
By the laws of consequence

The open arms of nature
All comers welcomed in
Rule for one, one rule for all
Neutral to virtue or sin

Free to come and free to go
To rape, pillage and plunder
But come the time she will slay
Without mercy lay asunder

And like all that came before
She holds the winning hand
The collective always aces
Each single step or strand.

Autumn Leaves

The autumn fields

So recently nurturing

Swathes of swollen, ripened, wholesome wheat

Now harrowed and naked

In the embarrassed dawn

Clinging like a startled monochrome maiden

To a veil of ghostly mist

Which sucks all colour from the air

'Til the waning warmth

Of the retiring sun

Lethargically drags it off

Revealing its own reflected, deflected splendour

In the falling honey-hued leaves

One by one, a descending arpeggio

To the welcoming earth

Soon to be re-consumed

In this random but perfectly ordered

Circle of life

A symphony whose exact notes

Will never be replayed again

But before this, they will lay

Gold on red on brown

Mottled, dappled, and satisfied

Giving up an unmistakable aroma
That fills the crisp still air
Thick and heady
A last hurrah
A signal that they will not be forgotten
They will be seen again.

Remember

A perfect lawn of men in green
Mown down blade by blade
A gentle thud
Heard only by the worm.
Fresh poppy-red blood
Turning dark maroon
No church bell chime
No time to prepare
Exhaled
Last wet breath of air
Expired
All too soon.
Contorted carcasses
In a heap

Lost hope
Lost dignity
Lost sheep
But your souls shall shine
For evermore
In fertile fields on high
Where no earthly roar
Will drown out your singing
In God's eternal sky.
'Til then, each and every November
If we take the time to stop and listen
We will hear you.
We will remember.

Don't Die on My Doorstep Please

It's a sign of the times what we worship
Seems like the mouse is mightier than the dove
The aged Star, Cross and Crescent
Struggle to compete with this new love
It'll soon have us all on our knees
Well, you can do your dying anywhere
But don't do it on my door step please

Shiny new goods are all electric
Costs driven down by arms of the strong
Skinny kids work in the mines for nothing
Life expectancy probably won't be long
Saving the planet won't save souls like these
Well, you can do your dying anywhere
But don't do it on my door step please

One man wins a million in a quiz show
Another million lost their crops to drought
Only one makes the paper's headlines
You can't be hurt by what you don't know about
So, there's no need to feel ill at ease
Well, you can do your dying anywhere
But don't do it on my door step please

Lady cuts the ad for a consultation
Ten thousand bucks for a lift might seem obscene
The next ad is placed by an eyesight charity
By a thousand bright new eyes she could be seen
Will we ever tackle this disease?
Well, you can do your dying anywhere
But don't do it on my door step please.

Trees

Twisted trunk of Umbrian olive
Taking goodness from parched soil
In an orchestra of magic
Transformed to a lustrous liquid oil

Camouflaged and peeling plane
Lining streets of the city
Leathery leaves scrub percussive air
Unnoticed. What a pity!

Gnarled bark of forest oak
So strong, no need for thorns
Piano birth of soft green saplings
From golden brown acorns

Giant redwood, ages old
One hundred metres tall
Queen of all that she surveys
Imperious over all

Sixty thousand species
Symbiotic harmony
Carbon marvels of our planet
Breath of life for you and me.

Seductive Nature

Clover mauve seduces the bumbling bees
Likewise, the bouquet of lilac wild thyme
Whilst fields of foxgloves and heartsease
Sirens singing as they please
Their come-and-get-me rhyme.

Atoms

Atoms, atoms everywhere
In the clouds and in your hair
Vibrant rainbow in the sky
Atoms in the planes that fly
Blood that courses through my veins
Water flowing down the drains
Atoms record my every thought
Atoms in the bread we bought
Pigments in our precious skin
Paint stirred in the artist's tin
In the fires of the sun
In the soldier's killing gun
Atoms form the mighty mountain

Lovers' coins lobbed in the fountain
Atoms in the forbidden apple
Sacred ceiling, Sistine chapel
Perpetual, steadfast yet so diverse
Throughout God's wondrous universe
In the galaxies' great black holes
But, I wonder, do we have atoms in our souls?

Days Gone By

Night's black cloak
Fell from the sky
And draped all form beneath
The thick soft cloth
Snuffed out still life
From heaven to the heath
And all the cast have disappeared
From this most tragic play
No tears are shed
And no-one mourns
The languid death of day

It's gone! It's gone!
It won't come back
Why's there no deep sorrow?
It's laid to rest
Did I do my best?
There's one less chance tomorrow.

Perfect State

When my bones are once more dust
And my blood has returned to the sea
Pure, immutable, preserved in trust
I shall forever be.

End of Part 1

Part 2.

Elements of the Mind
(Journey to a Void)

Where to start? None of us knows for sure what colours we each see and similarly what constitutes our thoughts.

But, as years go by, I realise that more people than I imagined have to wrestle with dark and light, those two forces within. Those two stubborn bedfellows who sometimes get along just fine but sometimes they just can't help but squabble.

I have come to understand this as an energy which needs some pretty careful management. When in equilibrium you wouldn't give it any mind, but it's potent and powerful when it tilts. What follows tries to throw some light on the darker side.

Full Moon

The delusion of the fullest moon
That mocks the sun
And lights my room
I stare into the darkness of the light
Exposed by the naked night
Paralysed by tricks and sleight
Mad thoughts in the gloom

A dozen covens of wailing witches
With lunar ticks
Scars and stiches
Piercing, howling, banshee cry
Lightning knives across the sky
Lock onto hypnotic eyes
Staring out from dingy ditches

No point, no purpose, these muses, wishes
Unlike the silent mice outside
Scurrying for snacks nutritious
Until, in turn, played foul
By the noble snow-white owl
Laser eye in downy jowl
Swoops with deathly swish

Ah, beauty in unfettered thought
Natural instinct
Not sold, not bought
No sauce, no season
No debate or reason
No plot, no treason
Just life and death that's aught.

Restless

Restless are the sands of a mighty desert dune
Restless are the flames that light the moon
Restless are the waves on the choppy sea
Restless are the winds that ruffle the tree
Restless are my thoughts in the still of night
Restless is my body taking flight
Agitated, fractious, fretful
Anxious, flustered, fitful
Restive, impatient, wild
Capricious, fidgety, child!
The consequence of being alive
The need to seek, the will to strive.

Trial

Every day is like a trial
Every inch seems like a mile
But I'm not hungry, I'm not cold
Will I be content before I'm old?
Oh, Lord please instil in me
The grace and wisdom just to be.

Tombstone

There's a vast grey sky
That's monumentally drab
Covering me up
Like a cold granite slab

For day after day
The wind is set from the east
The iron grip of gloom
Does not want me released

A lifeless landscape
A chill right down to the bone
Black boughs of the trees
Petrified monotone

Oh, for the presence
To think of time without pain
To see the sun rise
And infuse life again.

Out of Control

Out of control
On the helter-skelter
Bombs raining down on me
I'd go down in the air raid shelter
But it's dark down there
Nothing I can see

The water's rising
Slow but sure
Up to my neck,
Either way I'm done.
Is it so surprising?
What did I expect?

The deeper you go
The darker it gets
So scared to miss
Those unlocked doors
Along the labyrinth
Leading to the abyss

So, stop looking!
Hold your breath.
In order to find
Rise to the surface
Let go! Relax. Float,
To reclaim your mind

All will become clear
Light and whole
Unlock your ties
Safely supported
Infinite oceans of love
Now open your eyes

See the stars above
Stronger within
Each weight undone.
Believe, have faith
Certainty is easy
You're free to run

Paths and dead-ends
Shallows and deeps
In equal measure
Now calmly met
Able at last
To fully embrace life's treasure.

Whirlpool

Some people's lives seem plain sailing
Others, the passage is narrow and hard
When you can't walk or feel that you're failing
You're grasping at one bad luck card

They say clouds are lined with silver
They say light's at the end of the tunnel
What do they know about the waterway
That leads to this hopeless funnel?

To cross your Straits of Messina
You must avoid the monster called Scylla
Whose heads, like yours, are many but meaner
Whose limbs would wreck your flotilla

You may veer to ease your journey
You can't face any more torment today
A vision of your name on a gurney
Just waiting to whisk you away

In your haste to steer from danger
You feel a gentle pull from Charybdis
A mystical, schizophrenic stranger
Doom maiden or ultimate bliss?

At first her suction is welcome
Saving you from her sibling's harm
Her voice a musical, soporific strum
Words whispered with wide-open arms

You're tired and you cannot resist
The subtle speeding-up of the spiral
A swift sleight of hand, she writhes and she twists
So graceful, gleeful and gyral

Perhaps today you're not ready
To meet the whirlpool in all her glory
You try to fight the ebony eddy
Write more chapters in your story

But pass the event horizon
Imperceptible point of no return
You'll hear laughter from father Poseidon
In the distant heart of the churn

No matter how you set your sails
And no matter how hard you spin the wheel
Any attempt to change course sure to fail
A hidden hand has done the deal

Oh, shiny black swirling vortex
Please take me from my lugubrious gloom
Make simple all that makes life so complex
Draw me to the warmth of your womb

In the eye of her mad maelstrom
Charybdis sucks me to the underworld
Down past gates of fear and away from
Raining rocks, fury-fired and hurled

All pain may now be extinguished
With it the carousel of lows and highs
And all good things that you ever wished
To dry your watery eyes

But be careful, what's in your mind?
Imagining pain stops with your rebirth
Avoiding Scylla leaves tenfold behind
On the imperfect place called Earth.

I Wish

I wish I could have saved you
I wish I could have been there
I wish I would have called
And plucked you from despair
I wish lady luck had intervened
I wish the dice rolled kind
I wish the white horse rode away
And quelled your stormy mind
I wish I wasn't too busy
I wish I had been near
I wish all roads had not converged
At the vanishing point of the pier

I wish a thousand wishes
I wish them every day
I wish that time could be rolled back
But you're a million miles away
I wish that I could find you
I wish in some far-off land or sea
I can wish and wish and wish and wish
But it's just not meant to be.

- -

Numb

The clock has no hands
There's no more time
The drum beats mute
The bell's lost its chime
Meaning drifted out through an open door

I hear your voice
Inside my head
It's you who's gone
But I'm left for dead
Hands full of memories which turn to dust

I feel so numb
Yet feel such pain
Flicker of hope
Doused by torrential rain
That floods every corner of my soul

I call your name
There's no-one there
A bottomless void
Sorrow and despair
I never knew how dark dark could be

I see your prints
Upon the mirror
A cruel reminder
There was someone here
So close but impossible to reach

Like a careless fisher
With shredded nets
A troubled mind
And a thousand regrets
Sadly, you're the one that got away

Maybe to a place
That's fair and free
Somewhere far away
Beyond the deep blue sea
Protected from all hurt and harm at last

Until we meet again
My beautiful friend
All my earthly love
To you I send
Be patient and please save a space for me.

Other World

You walk down the road
Everyone's smiling
Bright blue skies
Song thrush singing
A beautiful tune beguiling
Harmonious and reconciled
But they're from the other world
You are the mother who had to bury her child

News on the radio
Headlines playing
Wars and politics
They're all talking
You don't know what they're saying
Noise immaculately compiled
But they're from another world
You are the mother who had to bury her child

Shops on the street
And shops online
Best ever deal
Make you look good
And make you feel fine
They've got it all stockpiled
But they're from another world
You are the mother who had to bury her child

Plane in the sky
Train at the station
Places to go
Schedules to meet
Must have a destination
Can't let it just run wild
But they're from another world
You are the mother who had to bury her child

Coffee shops
And take-away meals
Chitter chatter
But no-one knows
Just how it feels
To be forever exiled
But they're from the other world
You are the mother who had to bury her child.

Trial 2

Every day is like a trial
Every inch seems like a mile
I'm not hungry, I'm not cold
I have a home, I have some gold
Someone to talk to, someone to hold
And yet I yearn for something untold

Expecting a distant deathbed repentance
To provide parole from life's long sentence
But why wait 'til eternity to be free?
Oh, Lord, please instil in me
The grace and wisdom just to be.

Into the Void

Deep, dark, lugubrious liquid
Delicious, watery, glossy, galaxy
Spiralling, suction tentacle limbs
Irresistible, fluid force
Swirling and spinning me around
Hypnotising, paralysing
Drawing me ever closer
To the infinite whirlpool within
Jet black magnetic core
Threshold of no return
Voluptuous vortex void
Devourer of all worldly matters
With a Janus promise
Simultaneous safety and destruction.

Circuit breaker

The tension is hot
My nerves are on fire
The voltage is high
And keeps surging higher
How long can I hold
Before the circuits break?
I can't think clearly
There's too much at stake

Temperatures rising
I'm in the melting pot
Wires overloaded
How long have I got?
Black is the trickster
Infinity is dark
A false light of hope
From the crackling sparks

Time keeps on ticking
I'm a man out of time
A parallel world
No reason or rhyme
I wrestle control
To keep it inside
The harder I try
It just won't subside

I look for an outlet
A bolt of lightning
Its path can be random
Prospects are frightening
Fire and the fury
Trail of destruction
Relief or repentance
Cost of construction

I try to recall
The neutral switches
Deep sound of slow-down
Tranquilises twitches
A voice from within
Whispers "let it be"
Just lie there and float
When you're all at sea

Electrical storms
Transient and fickle
Blow themselves out
'Til the current just trickles
Don't feed them with fear
They mean you no harm
Wait for their passing
For rebirth and calm.

Be Calm

Let go, let go
Slow, slow, slow
Diffuse
Let the spring unwind
Be calm, becalm
No harm, don't harm
And inner peace you'll find.

- - - - - - - - - - - - - - - - - - - -

At the Fork

They say don't look back in anger
It does you no good
The die it was cast
In your childhood

When I clung to your apron ties
Was held in your arms
I felt only truth
In your home-spun charms

Then one day I rose up and left
And didn't think twice
In all certainty
There's a roll of the dice

I know I can doubt if this is
A dream or is real
I can see and touch
I can taste and feel

But can I really be so sure
The way that you were
That this is the truth
For him and for her?

Or did you understand too
That life is a mirror?
Passing to that side
You're really still here

But a mirror's for vanity
It captures the eye
So, when you turn round
The world has moved by

You've learned all you can
From the silence and talk
Go follow your instincts
When it comes to the fork.

True Dawn

Born in the dark hour
When the scar was not healed
As electrical storms
And green gargoyle forms
They screamed overhead
Where I buckled and kneeled

He longed to belong
To certainty past
Without the disorder
On twilight's border
No courage to summon
A solid iron cross cast

Present's the pinch point
Where the hourglass grains flow
A world crystallises
New dawn arises
What's to come has come
What's gone has yet to go

You stepped from within
A landscape of relief
With iridescent wings

An angel that sings
Fogs of confusion
Became rays of belief

Your silky hair brown
Like an artist's new brush
Eyes at once dark and bright
Make everything right
Seconds become hours
And peace supplants rush

So warm and so wide
Is your soft south sea smile
With lips rose petal pink
Perfect pearls that wink
Radiant beauty
Hope you'll stay here a while

As time ebbs and flows
Her constancy becalms
His wild ocean dreams
And fierce foaming schemes
Light over darkness
Cast by magical charms.

The Plough

I was never happier
Than when my hands were on the plough
The honesty of labour
The toil of here and now

Turning over day by day
Simple secrets of the earth
Studying stones holding sermons
Beholding seeds that give birth

But the evening sun is setting
And colours begin to fade
I look back into the twilight
At the things that I have made

I have an empty feeling
I can't relate to any one
And instead, I can't help thinking
Of all that's left undone

Places I never visited
And words I meant to say
Reconciliation notes unwritten
Finding that which went astray

And I wonder when it's dark
What'll be the notes that play
A dirge of deathly silence
Or fanfare for a brand-new day?

So, keep the furrows straight and true
Make the minimum of fuss
Feel the guiding hand of wisdom
Of what was forever thus

To fill your cup
You must surely drain another's
So only take what you need
And leave the rest for your brothers.

Path to Safety

When the storm clouds gather overhead
And darkness descends on me
You shine a light of hope
So that I might see
In the shadows of my mind
Where the mines of fear explode
You hold my hand and show me
It's a safe and harmless road.

End of Part 2

Part 3.

Elements of the Heart

The chemistry of emotion can take many forms. As stated in the introduction, I am a lucky man and have had the blessing of feeling both the slow-burn warmth and the more fickle, fiery heat of love.

This has given me much happiness but like any fire it needs tending to. Fan the embers to create a flame or let them turn to ash? Complacency is the damp, grey blanket hiding in plain sight and easy to succumb to. It takes some will-power to seek out the hot spots in the hearth, to recognise where the good embers glow and where the green wood might spit and burn.

I hope this section helps express that; venturing to the light and the shadowy places in our hearts, looking for the corners where angels might fly, which can be been a source for inspiration as well as understanding.

Journey Home

May strong winds be at your back
Warm sunshine caress your face
Your shadows far behind you
Steps of wisdom, steps of grace

Mountains high or valleys low
Or when your world's gone wrong
May your heart be light and willing
May your limbs be fit and strong

If clouds should mass above you
May their warm refreshing rain
Softly fill the gentle streams
That will wash away your pain

Darkest day or longest night
Let there be lights to guide the way
May there be a hand to hold
If fear forces you to stray

But when the journey's over
And the river's run its course
May your soul retain its beauty
Love brimming, eternal source.

Twenty Thousand Tides

Footloose and fancy free
Just seventeen you and me
When the cards were dealt
And we became a matching pair.
You're my earth
And I'm your moon
Not leaving your orbit anytime soon
Morning noon and night, you're always there

Lover, wife
Mother of life
Bearer of our children true and strong
Softly spoken gentle charms
Sweet smile and open arms
Together, forever, we belong

Market stall, coconut shy
Lazy eye might pass it by
But prise it open
And taste the sweetness of the milk.
Oyster shell
Mother of pearl
I can't believe that you're my girl
Mulberry bush provider for the silk

Lover, wife
Mother of life
Bearer of our children true and strong
Softly spoken gentle charms
Sweet smile and open arms
Together, forever, we belong

What was I looking for?
Cast iron love and molten core
Magnetic mistress
Always there to stop me going south.
See no flame
Feel the embers
Point the needle through December
Furnace heat draws a smile on my mouth

Lover, wife
Mother of life
Bearer of our children true and strong
Softly spoken gentle charms
Sweet smile and open arms
Together, forever, we belong

Something's shiny, fool's gold
Something darker might behold
Rubies, emeralds
Sapphires, diamonds, fit for Kings and Queens

Walnut burr
Bird's eye maple
Beneath the bark's a banquet table
I've been blessed to behold the unseen

Lover, wife
Mother of life
Bearer of our children true and strong
Softly spoken gentle charms
Sweet smile and open arms
Together, forever, we belong

I'm your storm you're my calm
Got my future in your palm
To my ebb and flow
You provide a rock-solid ground.
Unyielding
Unrelenting
One tough love that you're presenting
Like Themis, the fairest of them all

Lover, wife
Mother of life
Bearer of our children true and strong
Softly spoken gentle charms
Sweet smile and open arms
Together, forever, we belong

Hand in hand many a mile
Since we floated down that aisle
Joined through thick and thin
Spliced twenty thousand tides ago.
Bound by love
And laws of God
Side by side we're peas in a pod
You're for real girl, nothing is for show

Lover, wife
Mother of life
Bearer of our children true and strong
Softly spoken gentle charms
Sweet smile and open arms
Together, forever, we belong

Politicians' lies and wars
Nest of love behind closed doors
Battles rage outside
You're not changed by affairs of state.
Heart's at home
Heaven's above
Straight as an arrow, Cupid's love
I'll be there when we walk through those gates

Lover, wife
Mother of life
Bearer of our children true and strong
Softly spoken gentle charms
Sweet smile and open arms
Together, forever, we belong.

Swell

Like the restless ocean

Deep and dark and infinite

Shadows and moonlit glimpses

She ebbs and flows

Rises and falls

Swells

No edges

Just round, enveloping

Caressing, lapping

Peaks and troughs

Small waves, then foaming crests

Fury of curling, baying, breaking rollers

Up on hind legs

Baring all before
Smashing on the static shore
Sucking in unsuspecting stones
Down, down under
Cocooned in her irresistible current
Into the folds of salty safety
Played and rolled like dizzy dice
For a time known only to her
Gradually, remorselessly ground
Into a grain of sand
Over untold millennia
Sometime, somehow
To be spat back out on dry land
Like so many before
And so many yet to come
Giving, taking, shaping
To a hypnotic, perpetual sound
Constance, hiss, hush, slow, rush
Rhythmic strum or staccato scream
Whisper or a guttural roar
Always talking, calling the shots
Asking questions but silent in answer
And when it all subsides
Her lugubrious flow

Paralysing, pointless to protest

Will carry me away

Hapless, hopeless

I will breathe deeply and float once more

Becalmed as daybreak comes

And the respite of peace seeps in

A nirvana

A momentary suspension of time

Where to be is to forget.

————————————————

Blue

Blue, blue

Joy and sadness

The shades of love are blues

Her precious gemstone eyes

Look at me so coolly

Sparkling sapphire

And lapis lazuli

Windows to the soul of my muse

Blue, blue

Joy and sadness

The shades of love are blues

She walks in the forest

She lives amongst flowers

Heathers, bluebells
Combed rows of lavender
I am the bee your nectar woos

Blue, blue
Joy and sadness
The shades of love are blues
Her heart like an ocean
Mysterious and deep
Ultramarine
Then azure, then turquoise
Dissolving into different hues

Blue, blue
Joy and sadness
The shades of love are blues
With her web well woven
She calmly lures me in
Steel and neon
Powder and electric
Rising current to blow my fuse

Blue, blue
Joy and sadness
The shades of love are blues
So glad when she's around

67

So sad when she's away
Purple, violet
Baby blue, forget-me-not
My heart is so easy to bruise

Blue, blue
Joy and sadness
The shades of love are blues
Unwavering judgement
And established values
Cambridge, Oxford
Persian and Prussian too
On your scales I have paid my dues

Blue, blue
Joy and sadness
The shades of love are blues
A helpless prisoner
In a cell with no key
With midnight walls
And sky-blue barred glimpses
Of loving you I stand accused.

Red Sky Blues

Well the day's done driving through
Left a trail of dust in its wake
Well the day's done driving through
Left a trail of dust in its wake
In the morn the sun sets the sky on fire
It warns of the night-life that it takes

The streets start to fill with lovers
Everyone walking arm in arm
The streets start to fill with lovers
Everyone walking arm in arm
The heavens they twinkle in your eyes gal
And I'm falling for your moonbeam charms

Can't say if I'll be staying
So many things I need to do
Can't say if I'll be staying
So many things I need to do
Two days riding could see me in Venice
Or it could see me still here with you.

After the Windfall

It doesn't seem so long
Since she heard the sweet song
Of the lark as it sang in the sun
High on the air
That swelled the sweet pear
The cherry, strawberry and plum

For the fruit that was hers
She looks but defers
She can leave on the bough and forsake
Touched by dismay
As she sees it decay
And wonders what course she will take.

Bottle

He asked himself "What is the point?"
"Is this quenching my thirst?"
Moving onto another joint
Where the loser comes first

He went down in the French Quarter
A pitiful parade
Drinking with the rich man's daughter
A hollow renegade

From time to time he thinks of you
And wonders where you're at
Would you still share a point of view?
D'you wear a different hat?

The map lines are all well defined
Going from A to B
But when you're on the ground my friend
The world is full of trees

From side to side, up and down
On and off the throttle
You're out of time and out of place
Ship inside a bottle.

Unlocked

A free man sits alone in a room
Silent apart from the constant tick tock of the clock
Unable to move
But bound by what?
Apparently, nothing
Yet inside this soul the view is quite different
Invisible chains weigh heavy on his limbs
Each link cast in iron of unyielding insecurity

So strong, he often pulls and tugs to test them

Trying to find the limit without breaking

Glass walls, ceilings and floors

Constructed and hardened over time

From the shifting sands of his molten mind

Only visible to his touch

Impenetrable glazing, showing the sad prints of his hands

Where he has pressed up against to check

Nothing but this impossible divide separating him

From the Wurlitzer world beyond

A contained cauldron of frustration

Which boils over intermittently

Seeing places he wants to inhabit

But maybe these walls that are built for him

Are made by him for his protection

A barrier to life or death?

A lock on his heart

With no known key or combination

Made from an intricate web of restless thoughts

Woven over years of neglect

And fear that he is losing her

Vast doors of possibilities

Each one calling out with different temptations

With handles just out of reach

And yet none of this is real

If it's in the mind, is it?
One day he realises this and gets up
And decides to make the most
Of a world that is already his
To study it
To understand it
To find pleasure in it
To be sated
Content
At ease
Grateful
At which point the shackled energy
Dissipates and melts
Leaving him fresh and vital
His steps are unsteady
His mind unsure
The bright light overwhelming
A sea of noise drowning his thoughts
But instinct drives him on
Like a child he learns
Hungry
Inquisitive
Enquiring
A new world resolves itself
Until he looks back to see she is not with him

Her mouth moves silently

A look imploring

Pain and fear

Tears of rage

But she is bound by the same shackles

In the same glass box

There's no lock or key or path to return.

Border Crossing

He awoke and it was morning

And made for the door in a shaft of light

She turned and asked: What time is it?

He said: It's the end of the night

The beat of his boots on the floorboards sounded final

The feel of the brass handle the start of something new

She said: Don't be long boy

He said: Honey, you've never been so right

The motor fired up in the yard

Once the wheels had turned, he never looked back

The horizon kept unfolding

Sucking him down a path of pure black

Towns to the left and right with a world in every one
Worlds that only exist when you become part of them
But the past drove him on
Unswerving on this highway of tarmac

Noon the next day he reached the frontier
Eyes looking through a cheap kaleidoscope
Painted patchwork held in place by
Re-used rusty nails and fraying rope
Hawkers hovering everywhere, waiting for their prey
The sun beat down but his hat kept his cards in the shade
Concert of confusion
Connected by the common bond of hope

After six long nights he's in the clear
Standing on the edge of the market place
People trading bread and water
Sweeping down the steps and saying grace
Woman in a scarf looks at him like he's a stranger
She doesn't seem to know his heart's been here for a while
Unlike his memory
Which is still connected to another time and place.

Insatiable

A glass wall so thick yet so clear
He can hear you, see you
But can't smell, taste or touch you
He's so close but cannot get near
Simmering, smouldering
His heart's on fire
Nothing quells the flames
Or dampens the desire
Like a junkie with no money
Like a monkey with no honey
He can't stand or resist these games.

Dark Hole

There's a dark hole
Where your heart used to be
A cold void, vast and empty
With your bow ties
And your beau ties
With your better watch
And your better watch-out
With your fancy liquor
And your fancy licker
With your posh brogue
And your posh brogues

With your slick hair
And your slick air
With your champagne
And your sham pain
As I watch you bleed
I bleed like rain
A narcissistic love
But a deep self-loathing
When you look in the mirror
What do you see?
The man you are
Or the man you want to be?

Universal Laws

Sat in a chair that's flying through the air
Temporarily disconnected
Untethered and unprotected
From the land of my loved one
Whose lure is as strong as
Mother Earth who is pulling me home

Going round a globe that's going round a sun
A lone star among trillions sublime
Waltzing their way through space and time
Suspended swirling spirals
Gigantic great whirlpools
Ev'ry atom obeying the rules

How can this be from the small to the large?
Men with telescopes and teaspoon thoughts
Trying to explain with ones and noughts
From the point it all began
To the end of time itself
Asking themselves "What *is* the matter"?

A universal chain, no links broken
Gravity apple and rainbow prism
United in purpose, no schism
From here to infinity
In the heavens above
But do they know the formula for love?

Tell me wise sir, have you yet cracked the code?
Can you measure it and then weigh it?
Can you dissect or display it?
Can you bottle it for me?
Ferment it by degrees?
With one of your marvellous machines

You and I are on the same long journey
But perhaps both searches are in vain
Neither may we fully explain
The more we find out about
The more we can't fathom
The more we grasp, the more we let go

So, I return from this heavenly muse
Flighty bird of possibility
Meets hard ground of reality
Darkness looms, cast by the sun
Draped over the earth's folds
The object comes to meet its shadow

Perhaps the light will come not from the dark
But from a place that's buried inside
Closed to all those who vainly tried
Which reason extinguishes
But which hope can alight
Be content that to feel *is* to know

You, Aphrodite and Venus in one
With your myrtle oil and turtle dove
Well you knew where there lives true love
Laugh at me the busy fool
Come now to realise
Full circle like the stars, found at last.

Seven Seas Apart

The sails on this ship are ripped
The ropes are frayed
The cargo's flipped
The captain is all at sea
But he's still sailing

Because he's in love with you
And there's nothing
He wouldn't do
To get to the horizon
Without capsizing

Forty days and forty nights
Albatross hopes
And stars for lights
Tastes the salt upon his lips
All cracked and broken

One more wrench on the rudder
The listing ship
Groans and shudders
Ploughing on through endless waves
Shaped by fate's four winds

For too long I've been roaming
Wild white horses
Whipped and foaming
I need your land 'neath my feet
And you around me

Gentle warmth of your embrace
Your silky skin
And loving face
Thoughts that make my spirits lift
My heart's a-pounding

I'm not to know when we'll meet
Cross in my hand
Knelt at your feet
Your hands placed upon my head
Whispered vows of love

But 'til the hour our flags raise
I'll fight it out
These doldrum days
Hatches battened and heart locked
Seven seas apart.

Fire and Fury

Fiery furnace
Searing heat
Feelings forged
Make me complete

Stoke the embers
Wood and coal
You light the fires
Of my soul

Blue and orange
Reds and yellows
Fan the fames
Pump the bellows

Wrought iron rose
Perfect petals
Thorns of gold
Precious metals

Molten rocks
Loving ladle
Dipped and spooned
On our table

Hardened anvil
Hammer and tongs
Rhythmic beat
Cast iron songs.

Three's a Crowd

Shut the door
Pull down the blind
Come sit with me
And free your mind.
Uncork that bottle
Heady red wine
Soft rhythms of soul
It'll all be fine.
Mystical woman
Magical empress
Black and white pearls
Perpetual priestess.
And breathe again
Heaven's stars above
Celestial bodies
Backdrop for love.
Candlelight shadows
On a calico shroud
I think we're agreed
Three's a crowd.

I Am. And You Are

I am. And you are.
Together we'll drive this beat up car
Till the road runs out
Or the wheels fall off
Or the motor fires no more.
How steep the mountain
How deep the vale
How high the fountain
How intoxicating the trail
How much spirit we burn
How many twists and turns
However far it will be
Will be far enough for you and me.
Wherever it takes us
We'll get to wherever whenever
It's our destiny
Content to want what we have
Not have what we want
We'll embrace this ride
Hand in hand
Side by side
Together we'll stand
The unknown test of time.

- - - - - - - - - - - - - - - - - - - -

Complete

It's the little things you do
That do it for me
You think that I don't notice
But actually, I see.

Seconds may make hours
And days may make a year
But it's the little things you do
That keep me staying near
Seeds may form fine flowers
Raindrops may fill an ocean
But it's the little things you do
That's your secret loving potion
It takes steel to build a bridge
And silk to weave fine lace
But it's the little things you do
That put a smile upon my face
It's the stars that shine in heaven
And the sun that gives us heat
But it's the little things you do
That make me feel complete.

Journey (reprise)

May strong winds be at your back
Warm sunshine caress your face
Your shadows far behind you
Steps of wisdom, steps of grace

Mountains high or valleys low
Or when your world's gone wrong
May your heart be light and willing
May your limbs be fit and strong

If clouds should mass above you
May their warm refreshing rain
Softly fill the gentle streams
That will wash away your pain

Darkest day or longest night
Let there be lights to guide the way
May there be a hand to hold
If fear forces you to stray

But when the journey's over
And the river's run its course
May your soul retain its beauty
Love brimming, eternal source.

End of Part 3.

Also by John Deed:

The A to Z of Country Limericks

A light-hearted collection of nonsense rhymes, with vibrant and engaging cartoon illustrations by Sean MacGarry, suitable for all ages.

One country is covered for each letter of the alphabet (including a little poetic licence when we get to "X"!). These limericks primarily aim to amuse, but with an additional sprinkling of interesting facts about each country "visited", they might also stimulate the enquiring mind.

The countries for each verse were chosen for their rhyming possibilities and range from some very well-known ones such as France and Spain to some lesser-known places such as Angola and Oman.

Purchase softback or Kindle at:

amazon.co.uk or amazon.com

or find out more at:

flyingpigments.co.uk

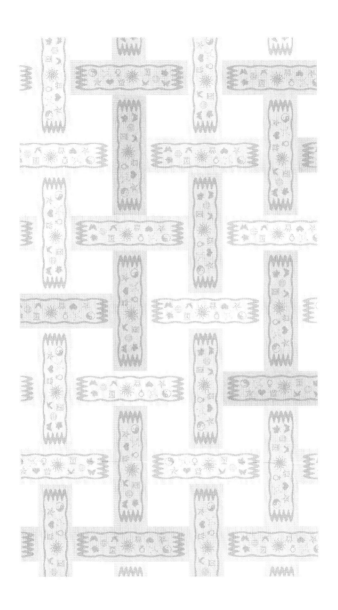

91

Printed in Great Britain
by Amazon